Original title:
A Symphony of Sprouts

Copyright © 2025 Creative Arts Management OÜ
All rights reserved.

Author: Simon Fairchild
ISBN HARDBACK: 978-1-80581-919-6
ISBN PAPERBACK: 978-1-80581-446-7
ISBN EBOOK: 978-1-80581-919-6

Nature's Flourishing Fanfare

In the garden, things are spry,
Carrots wiggle, onions sigh.
Peas are poking, oh so bright,
As radishes dance in pure delight.

Bouncing beans in a jolly race,
Broccoli wears its crown with grace.
Lettuce laughs in shades of green,
While squashes flaunt their boisterous sheen.

The Euphony of Edibles.

Tomatoes giggle, ripe and round,
In the patch, a funny sound.
Cucumbers sliding down the vine,
Zucchini jokes with a twist of lime.

Garlic whispers, 'What a flair!'
While chives peek from their comfy lair.
Radishes take a leafy bow,
"Let's party!" shouts the sprout, "and now!

Whispers of Green Harmony

Spinach sings a leafy tune,
Kale joins in, a funky boon.
Herbs are swaying, feeling spry,
Oregano waves to the passersby.

Celery's cracking silly jokes,
While peas perform their playful pokes.
Cabbage rolls in cozy pride,
As peppers dance, side by side.

Melodies Beneath the Soil

Roots are tapping, making sound,
Underneath, they twirl around.
Carrots chuckle, potatoes grin,
"Let's dig deep and host a win!"

Earthworms wiggle, having fun,
Playing games 'til day is done.
Garden gnomes sit, amused by all,
As laughter echoes through the hall.

Voices of the Sprouted Earth

In the garden, whispers play,
Tiny seeds have much to say.
With a giggle, they will sprout,
Telling tales that swirl about.

Worms are dancing in a line,
Beneath the leaves, they feel divine.
While daisies gossip, stretched with glee,
Sharing dirt, as carefree as can be.

Sunbeams tickle every bud,
Silly ants march in the mud.
Laughter echoes in the breeze,
As sprouts wiggle 'neath the trees.

Look at them, their party grand,
Party hats made from the land.
Nature's jesters bloom so bright,
In a world of pure delight.

Nature's Lyric in Full Bloom

Petals flap like tiny birds,
In the breeze, they sing in words.
While carrots clash their orange tops,
The radishes perform their hops.

Cauliflower struts in a tutu,
With sprigs of green, it feels brand new.
Tomatoes chuckle, plump and red,
While lettuce whispers secrets fed.

Butterflies call for a dance,
Nature's players in a trance.
The rhythm's swell is oh so sly,
As veggies twirl and mushrooms fly.

Each petal plays a frolic tune,
Beneath the watchful, winking moon.
And in this patch, with laughter bright,
Every sprout's a pure delight.

Lyrical Landscape of the Growing Season

In fields where joy and green collide,
Beans and peas take fun-filled rides.
With sprout-like giggles all around,
Their silly songs are joy unbound.

Sunflowers wear their crowns so tall,
While broccoli stands proud, though small.
They wave and sway, a merry crew,
In a garden party, fresh and new.

The radishes break into a jig,
While mushrooms chat and dance a fig.
Zucchinis strum on leafy strings,
As the merry earth-life sings.

Silly squirrels sneak in for cheese,
While flowers sway with utmost ease.
All nature's players join the scene,
In this humorous, leafy green.

The Dance of Life and Light

Underneath the sun's warm glow,
Tiny sprouts put on a show.
With a wiggle and a twist,
Growing things can't be dismissed!

The daisies laugh as they recline,
And share their dreams of summer wine.
Some lettuce asks for a dance break,
While peas jump high, oh for goodness' sake!

High on stems, the daisies cheer,
Saying, "Look at us, we've got no fear!"
Cabbages roll and then they spin,
In this veggie-funny din.

Even dandelions blow their fluff,
Saying, "We're too cute, that's enough!"
Each sprout's a comic in disguise,
Beneath the wide and laughing skies.

A Garden's Harmonious Awakening

In the soil, roots do tango,
Carrots waltz, it's quite a show!
Beets are blushing, oh so bright,
While peas are giggling, what a sight!

The radishes, they throw confetti,
Lettuce's head spins, feeling petty.
Tomatoes bounce to the beat,
Cucumbers groove on little feet!

Sunflowers pop their heads on high,
"Look at us!" they wave, oh my!
While onions cry big salty tears,
"Do we smell good?!" They share their fears.

In the patch, laughter's grown and spread,
Nature's fun, a dance instead!
No need for music, just embrace,
The joyous rhythm of this place!

Interlude of the First Blossoms

Here comes spring, with all its flair,
Daffodils dance without a care.
Tulips twirl, with colors bright,
Petunias chirp, a funny sight!

The daisies hop in a small parade,
Sunshine rays, their grand charade.
Pansies wear the silliest grin,
"Is it time to bloom, let's begin!"

Lilies lunge in a mad dash,
"Water us, not make a splash!"
The gardener checks, with eyes so wide,
"Oops! Tripped on a petal!" he sighed.

But in this chaos, joy elopes,
With every bloom, a tale of hopes.
So laugh along as petals cheer,
Springtime's antics, oh so dear!

Nature's Rhythmic Unfolding

In a glade where critters dwell,
Bumblebees buzz, oh what a spell!
The ants in line, they march and boast,
"Who needs a map? We know our coast!"

Under leaves, a frog does croak,
"Hey, have you heard the latest joke?"
While dragonflies zip here and there,
"Catch us, if you dare, fair and square!"

Grasshoppers strum on blades of green,
"Join our band, let's make a scene!"
While crickets chirp a rhythm fine,
"Beware! Our song is hard to define!"

Nature hums a silly tune,
From dawn's light to the glow of moon.
So join the fun, don't be shy,
In the wild, let laughter fly!

Flourish in a Delicate Balance

A butterfly lounges, sipping dew,
Spilling tales of gardens anew.
"Hear the whispers of the daisies,"
As they chatter, a bit too crazy!

The heron strikes a pose so bold,
"Look at me, I'm such a gold!"
While squirrels argue about the stash,
"He took my acorn, what a clash!"

The sun and moon, they play tag light,
"Catch me if you can, what a sight!"
The stars chime in with twinkling cheer,
"What's this ruckus? We want to hear!"

In this balance of chaos and grace,
Life's a jest, a giggly race.
So tip your hat, and take a bow,
In nature's jest, let laughter wow!

Choreography of the Seed

In the garden, seeds take a bow,
They shimmy and shake, oh wow!
Tiny dancers in the soil,
Each one ready to uncoil.

Roots twist like they're on the floor,
While leaves fly high, who could ask for more?
With sunlight as their disco ball,
They groove and jig—it's a ball!

Sprouts pop up in a comical spree,
Striking poses, look at me!
Some lean left, some sway right,
All beneath the sky so bright.

The weeds take red cards, they're out,
While sprouts giggle, twist, and shout.
Every bud a superstar,
Nature's stage, oh, how bizarre!

Nature's Crescendo of Growth

Tiny sprouts rise with a cheer,
Growing faster, oh so clear!
They stretch and yawn, flexing to the sky,
While dandelions giggle nearby.

Each leaf plays a note so bold,
In the orchestra of green and gold.
Roots hum the bass, steady and deep,
While birds in crowns... well, they just peep!

The sun beams down, crackling with cheer,
Flowers pop out, resolving that fear.
An encore of colors, a vibrant show,
Nature's giggle, from below!

So gather 'round, come see the fun,
When nature grows, the wackiness has begun!
With every plant, a story to unfold,
These green musicians are fierce and bold!

Harmonies of Leaf and Root

Leaves whisper secrets, roots laugh loud,
Together they form a quirky crowd.
With every gust, they dance in chat,
Twirling to the tunes of a ladybug's hat.

Each stem knows just the right groove,
Pulsing along to the photosynthesis move.
Tickling the soil like a friendly breeze,
They sway together with playful ease.

Sunshine's applause rains from above,
While ants march in, they're ready to shove.
In this playful garden, there's never a frown,
Just leafy giggles and roots painted brown!

Every sprout has its part to play,
In this comical, green cabaret.
A leaf flutters down, says "What's your plan?"
"Just grow and joke!" says the tiny man.

Vibrations from the Underground

Down below, there's a riotous cheer,
Where roots wiggle, that's quite clear.
Moles join in, some tap their toes,
While worms bust moves, in fancy clothes!

The soil hums a lively tune,
With fungi adding a funky boon.
"Let's dig deeper," the carrots insist,
As beets give a wink, "We can't be missed!"

Symphonies play in the mud so deep,
The radishes cheer; they can't help but leap.
Little critters rock the dirt jam,
As seeds laugh, "Look, I'm going ham!"

So if you listen, down in the earth,
You'll hear a party, celebrating birth.
With roots strumming tight, and all of them sprout,
Just a nutty world, full of fun, there's no doubt!

The Lullaby of Leafy Greens

In gardens where the cabbages sway,
They dance with joy on sunny days.
Lettuce giggles, radishes wink,
Together they grow, no time to think.

Tomatoes blush in their crimson shirts,
While peas whisper secrets in tiny flirts.
Zucchini jokes about being long,
In this patch, nothing feels wrong.

Melodic Echoes of the Growing Season

Roots tap-dance beneath the soil,
While sprouts begin their dance and toil.
Carrots snicker with a cheeky grin,
Saying, 'Come at us, we won't give in!'

Cucumbers stretch in their fancy vines,
Raspberries sing sweet and tangy lines.
Each plant plays its quirky part,
Creating a tune that warms the heart.

Seasons of Green Enchantment

Spring arrives on a giggly breeze,
Tickling petals, making trees tease.
Beans skip about in playful rows,
They laugh as they gently impose.

Summer brings a juicy cheer,
As melons roll and shed a tear.
Pumpkins sit with plump delight,
Saying, 'We're shy, but oh, what a sight!'

Nature's Musical Transitions

Autumn rustles leaves that jive,
With squash singing, 'We're so alive!'
Each kernel pops and starts to dance,
As squirrels gather with hungry prance.

Winter whispers, 'Don't be meek!'
Spinach grins at a chilly peak.
Frosty hums a chilly tune,
While veggieland dreams of sun and moon.

The Hidden Orchestra of Roots

Deep down below, a concert's begun,
Wiggly worms jam, having so much fun.
The beetles all dance, on tiptoes they prance,
As roots hold the beat, in their earthy romance.

A celery flute plays, the carrots drumbeat,
While radishes waltz with a curious beet.
The underground gnats buzz a lively refrain,
In this hidden band, there's no chance of pain.

Leaves sway on top, in rhythm with glee,
Tiny sprigs tapping, "Join the jubilee!"
While ants with their snacks, take a front row seat,
With tattered old hats, they keep the groove neat.

So if you should wander in fields near and wide,
Remember the music of friends that abide.
With roots below, they'll never miss out,
A hidden extravaganza, without any doubt!

Leafy Lullabies

In the hush of the garden, leaves softly hum,
Whispers of laughter, a natural drum.
The daisies and dandelions take center stage,
Each one a performer, no matter the age.

The broccoli sings with a croaky refrain,
While lettuce sways lightly, "Feel free to gain!"
Chorus of petals, a soft leafy choir,
Serenading the moon with whimsical fire.

Buds twirl and twinkle in soft evening air,
Each note made of green, a whimsical flair.
With crickets as backup, strumming their strings,
Even old toads join with ribbeting things!

So stroll through the glade, if you need a smile,
The leafy lullabies stretch for a while.
In shadows of gardens, where laughter's alive,
Nature's sweet melodies help dreams to thrive.

Blossoms in Full Flourish

Petals pop open, a colorful spree,
Racing each other in a flowery sea.
The roses are twirling, in pinks and in reds,
While tulips in yellow bounce straight from their beds.

A daffodil giggles, its trumpet held high,
As indigo irises play peek-a-boo spry.
Each blossom unfurls, with joy in their throats,
Making sure the garden is in full float.

"Watch out for bees," yells the shy little bud,
"Dance quick, my dear friends, don't land in the mud!"
A melody blooms in the bright sunlight's rays,
As blooms take their bows, on this fine spring day.

So let's leap and twirl in this radiant scene,
As flowers unite in a fun, lively sheen.
With laughter and color, they cheerfully rush,
In a world full of petals, pure joy's in the lush.

Nature's Rising Aria

In the brightening morn, a song starts to rise,
With chirps and with chuckles, under blue skies.
That chubby old robin has taken the lead,
While squirrels hold the notes, with acorns to feed.

A chorus of critters, each plays their own way,
The crickets are buzzing, it's lively today!
As flowers sway lightly, in rhythm they sway,
Nature's got talents, come join the ballet.

The wind is a dancer, whirling with flair,
Tickling the petals, with music to share.
Though sunshine is bright, the shadows all play,
As lighthearted breezes chase old clouds away.

So gather your friends, let's all sing along,
In fields where the laughter grows buoyant and strong.
Nature's grand aria lifts spirits so high,
With giggles and joy that float up to the sky.

Harmonizing the Growth Cycle

In the garden, things are spry,
Tiny seeds that dance and fly.
With a wiggle and a sway,
They greet the sun, hip-hip-hooray!

Little roots dive deep, go bold,
Planting dreams in soil so gold.
A leaf sneezes, oh so loud,
While bugs cheer, they're feeling proud!

With carrots dressed in leafy flair,
And radishes with rosy hair.
The peas play tag among the dirt,
While lettuce laughs, it's quite a flirt!

In this patch, where fun's the rule,
Every sprout thinks it's a jewel.
Join the dance, let laughter bloom,
Nature's party in full plume!

A Quiet Evolution of Green

In the silence, sprouts awake,
Sharing secrets as they shake.
A cabbage wears a leafy crown,
While the carrots giggle, oh so brown.

The garlic whispers, 'Keep it sweet!'
While sleepy potatoes tap their feet.
Basil breathes in sunshine's glow,
And says, 'Let's put on a show!'

As the beans begin to climb,
They stretch to reach the clouds, oh my!
Sunflowers tall, with heads held high,
Make sure to wave as bugs pass by.

Underneath the sky so blue,
Each sprout knows just what to do.
With every laugh and every cheer,
Nature's evolution, oh so dear!

Undercurrents of Life's Melody

In the dirt, where giggles play,
Worms create a wiggly ballet.
Tiny sprouts reach for the breeze,
While wearing tiny polka-dots with ease.

A tomato blushes, feeling bold,
While radishes spin tales of old.
Zucchini tells a joke, quite sly,
As butterflies flutter by to pry.

The garlic chants a funky beat,
With every root, they get up on their feet.
The peas are rolling in a heap,
In this garden, joy runs deep.

As bees zoom in to join the jam,
The garden whispers, "Oh, slam-bam!"
With leaves that giggle in delight,
Life's melody dances in the light!

Flora Enchanted by Sunlight

Oh, the flowers twirl and spin,
Each petal grinning with a grin.
They bask beneath the golden ray,
Swaying gently, come what may.

The daisies gossip, "What a day!"
While tulips blush in bright display.
A sunflower strikes a pose so grand,
Trying hard to start a band.

The beans chatter about their height,
Complaining 'bout the bird in flight.
"Oh no! Not a pecking spree!"
A scarecrow joins, 'Just leave it to me!'

In this plot where laughter thrives,
Each sprout knows how to come alive.
With sunlight kisses and gentle fun,
The garden hums; oh, what a run!

Nature's Growing Orchestra

In the garden, ants do dance,
Puppets in a green expanse.
They twirl and spin with tiny feet,
A burst of joy, oh what a treat!

Bees buzz loud, and worms do waddle,
Proudly showing off their noddle.
While daisies sway, a floral cheer,
Each petal waving, 'Spring is here!'

With every sprout, the giggles bloom,
As carrots tease from underground gloom.
The radishes burst in fiery red,
Dreaming of salads, dance in their bed!

Nature's choir, a motley crew,
Performing in rain, sun, and dew.
They laugh and play, in leafy glee,
An orchestra of green, oh what a spree!

The Unseen Cadence

Underneath, the roots all tap,
With beats so slick, like a rhythm map.
Whispers of clover, secrets told,
A jazz of greens, both brave and bold.

Earthworms croon a low bass tune,
While fungi hum beneath the moon.
A sprinkle here, a wiggle there,
Nature grins, 'Join us if you dare!'

With every seed, a quirk unfolds,
The lettuce dreams of tales retold.
Peas gather round, the punchline's near,
"Green thumbs up, we're all in here!"

Squirrels laugh from their lofty perch,
As they watch the kale do its lurch.
A jig of joy in the garden bed,
Nature's cadence, lightly tread!

Songs of the Sprouting Cycle

In the soil, a party brews,
Tiny sprouts with silly views.
They shout, "Look at us, we're sprouting wide!"
As they reach for the sky, full of pride!

Sunflowers giggle, tall and bright,
Waving to the clouds in delight.
While lettuce waves, a cheeky grin,
Come dance with us, let the fun begin!

Radishes hop and onions sing,
All amongst the blossoming spring.
Carrots pipe in with their own tune,
"We're the cool kids, join us soon!"

Nature's band, a playful crew,
Crafting songs of the fresh and new.
With roots and leaves as their best friends,
The cycle spins, and laughter blends!

The Language of Leaf and Stem

In whispering leaves, secrets hum,
As sprouts emerge, they swish and thrum.
"Hey, did you hear? A sunflower's shy!"
"Not as shy as that broccoli by and by!"

Petunias prattle, in colors loud,
While peppers boast, "Look at our crowd!"
"Let's have a chat about the rain,"
"Oh yes, let's sprout, forget the pain!"

The daisies giggle in vibrant cheer,
"Let's plan a party for all to hear!"
With roots connecting, laughter flows,
In the garden, anything goes!

So join the dance, where leaves can swing,
And celebrate the joy of spring!
Nature speaks in its own fun way,
A language rich, bright as the day!

Crescendo of New Life

In the garden, a seed took a dance,
It wiggled and jiggled, given a chance.
With a kick and a spin, it rose from the dirt,
Wearing a leaf like a tiny green shirt.

The carrots are grinning, the radishes cheer,
Glancing at sprouts that are growing near.
They're having a party under the sun,
With a splash of water, oh what fun!

The tomatoes are giggling, bursting with pride,
While the onions are crying, they just can't hide.
A lavender tune floats through the air,
As the daisies dance without a care.

Through the tangle of vines and roots they play,
Pretending the weeds are the stars of the day.
The earth gives a chuckle, a twist, and a spin,
Celebrating life with a cheeky grin!

Echoes in the Garden

Listen closely, hear the plants hum,
Each little sprout creates a soft drum.
The sunflowers sway, conducting the show,
While the cucumbers giggle as they grow.

The beans have a chorus, singing away,
With peas in a pod that join for the play.
A zucchini croons tunes, feeling so spry,
With the mighty oak's whispers floating by.

The carrots tap dance, their roots in the ground,
While beets with their friends spin round and round.
Petunias flutter like butterflies bright,
In this botanical band, such a cute sight!

So if you feel down, just visit this place,
Where nature composes with flair and with grace.
With laughter and joy, the plants serenade,
In a garden of music, memories made.

Tuning the Earth's Orchestra

In the dirt, an ensemble begins to align,
With potatoes joining in, claiming divine.
Carrots pluck strings, with rhythm and cheer,
While tomatoes sound horns that everyone can hear.

The radishes hum a low, mellow tune,
As sunlight casts shadows beneath the bright moon.
Cucumbers strum with a crisp, crunchy sound,
In this underground concert where magic is found.

Lavender scents waft and sway in the breeze,
Creating a harmony that puts hearts at ease.
Each sprout has a role, in joyful array,
In this garden of laughter where sprouting plants play.

So come lend your ears, hear the roots and the leaves,
In this big band of blooms, everyone believes.
The Earth plays a melody, rich and so bright,
A tune of pure joy that dances in light!

The Rhythm of Growing Things

The basil is tapping its tiny green feet,
While the broccoli boogies to a funky beat.
Cauliflower twirls in a fluffy white skirt,
The rhythm of greens all dancing in dirt.

Radishes roll like little red balls,
And lettuce flutters as springtime calls.
Dancing between rows, they shake and they sway,
In the garden's parade on this beautiful day.

The peppers all whistle, with jalapeños in line,
Leeks laugh and giggle, feeling so fine.
Spinach sings softly, with a whispering breeze,
In a garden concert that aims to please.

So join in the fun, in this plot full of cheer,
Where each sprout's a star, and the laughter is near.
With soil as our stage and sun as our light,
We'll dance through the day and groove through the night!

The Forest's Quiet Chorus

In the woods where small things play,
Tiny leaves dance night and day,
Whispers of critters fill the air,
Jumping jays sing without a care.

Acorns roll like natural drums,
Squirrels prance, and giggle, and hums,
Beneath the boughs, the laughter grows,
As nature's joy in silence flows.

Mice with maracas in their paws,
Chirp along with nature's laws,
A woodpecker snaps the beat in time,
While rabbits hop in rhythm, sublime.

So join the fun, oh whimsical trees,
And sway to the tunes of the buzzing bees,
For in this grove where silliness busts,
A chorus of sprouts is full of trusts.

Reviving the Melodic Landscape

Seeds took a nap and woke with glee,
Swaying in tune, oh can't you see?
Grasshoppers strum their legs with flair,
While flowers shimmy without a care.

A ladybug waltzes on a leaf,
Tickled by winds, she's quite the thief,
Stealing the show in colors bright,
As crickets chirp into the night.

Bees hum a tune to nature's chat,
Inviting ants to join the spat,
With petals flapping like they're in a race,
Nature's garden, a dizzy place.

Roots stomp beneath, wanting their share,
While branches wiggle up in the air,
With every sprout, a brush of fun,
Nature's party has just begun!

Uplifted by Gentle Breezes

Whispers of wind tease the shoots,
As they bounce in their tiny boots,
Ticklish breezes prance and swirl,
As daffodils giggle and twirl.

Sunbeams beam down, a golden host,
As butterflies flutter, they love the most,
They tumble around like playful fools,
Over the garden's sparkling jewels.

Clouds drift by in a silly race,
While green sprouts beam with a sunny face,
Dancing to a tune that's soft, yet spry,
Chasing sunlight across the sky.

In this land where sprouts come alive,
All together, they do thrive,
With every gust, they laugh and leap,
For joy flows here, so wild and deep.

Ode to Nature's Unseen Hands

Oh, tiny gardener in the ground,
With every poke, new sprouts are found,
With mischievous smiles, they wave hello,
Through soil rich, their giggles flow.

Worms till the soil, a helpful crew,
While critters plan what they might do,
With snickers and chirps, they plot and scheme,
Unseen hands weaving a funny dream.

Rabbits wear hats made of branches bright,
As mushrooms pop up, quite a sight,
Imaginations sprout with glee,
Creating mischief for all to see.

In gardens where whimsy knows no end,
Nature plays tricks like a playful friend,
So here's to the hands, so clever and grand,
That nurture the joy in our laughing land.

The Dance of the Tender Shoots

Little shoots in a sprightly jig,
Twisting and twirling, they'd all dig.
With tiny leaves fluttering all about,
They stomped the ground and let out a shout!

Sunlight beams, their little guide,
Bouncing up, down, they just can't hide.
A worm joins in with a curious sway,
Spinning in circles, come join the play!

In the garden, such joyful noise,
The ants join in, they're tiny but poised.
The daisies giggle, petals a-flutter,
While raindrops dance like they're made of butter!

So who said sprouts can't be a blast?
In this garden party, you'll have a blast!
With every sprout in a dance so fun,
Join in the rhythm, for everyone!

Echoes of Vitality

Listen close, the sprouts sing loud,
With giggles rising, they form a crowd.
Each tiny leaf, a legend untold,
Of mischief and magic in sunshine bold!

They whisper secrets to the breeze,
A chorus of chuckles beneath the trees.
A beetle plays drums on a soil-strewn log,
While roots tap dance like a lively frog!

The carrots chuckle, buried so deep,
While sunflowers sway, in rhythm they leap.
A funky fungus joins the beat,
With all of nature ready to greet!

So let every sprout in this green parade,
Shout out their story, don't be afraid!
For echoes of life, both silly and spry,
Bring forth a laughter that never will die!

Petals in Perfect Pitch

Petals dance to the tunes of the breeze,
Swirling around with such effortless ease.
Daisies are soloists, bold and bright,
Singing their hearts out, oh what a sight!

Tulips join in, a colorful crowd,
Each note they sing, startlingly loud.
A butterfly conductor, with flair and style,
Leads the performance, making us smile!

From buds that bloom to blooms that fall,
They laugh and twirl, having a ball.
The wind's gentle waltz brings laughter anew,
As nature hums softly, a sweet little tune!

So gather around, hear this cheerful choir,
With wildflower symphonies lifting you higher.
In gardens of laughter, where aromas blend,
A melody sprouted, where giggles ascend!

The Flourishing Chorus

In whispers of green, a chorus arose,
With leafy voices, they struck a pose.
Roots in a line like they're ready to sing,
While playful buds bounce on a spring!

Chickadees chuckle from high on a branch,
As sprouts sway low in a giggly dance.
The soil gives a groan as they leap very high,
"Earthquake!" they holler, but it's just a spry!

The tulip's a star, with a voice that glows,
While the veggies below hum their leafy prose.
The radishes rustle, in harmony swell,
Joining the fun, as they weave a tale well!

So let's join the laughter beneath the blue sky,
With blooming friendships that never run dry.
Here in the garden, there's never a bore,
Through laughter and lyrics, we always want more!

Ballad of the Budding World

In a garden where beet greens dance,
Radishes prance in a funny romance.
Tiny sprouts with their silly hats,
Wiggling side to side like little cats.

The peas are peeking, oh what a sight,
Telling each other, 'We're veggies tonight!'
Carrots giggle from under the ground,
'Look up and see our green friends abound!'

Lettuce laughs, 'I'm feeling so crisp!'
While broccoli dreams of a superhero wisp.
Together they sing, a comical tune,
As daisies sway beneath the bright moon.

From tomato to onion, the fun will not end,
In the realm of the sprouts, all are best friends.
With every new sprout that decides to appear,
The garden's a circus—the laughter is here!

Serenade of the Sprouting Season

When spring arrives, the seeds take a peek,
Saying, 'Let's grow up, it's time to be cheek!'
The daisies are gossiping over their tea,
'Who wore it better, you or me?'

Tiny tomatoes in a conga line,
Wiggling their roots, feeling just fine.
Zucchini smiles, 'I'm the king of the patch!'
While peppers joke, 'We're ready to hatch!'

Carrots are plotting a game of charades,
While cucumbers dodge under leafy cascades.
'Can you guess what I am?' the onions tease,
As they stand there, swaying in the breeze.

With laughter and sproutlings all mixed in a swirl,
The garden erupts with a bright, sunny twirl.
So raise up your forks and join in the fun,
For sprouting season has only begun!

Cacophony of Colors in Bloom

Sunflowers wear shades that are quite outlandish,
While violets compete to see who is brandish.
In a riot of colors, they giggle and cheer,
Each bloom a character joining the sphere.

The daisies shout, 'Look at us leap!'
As they try to outdo each other in sleep.
Buttercups chuckle, 'We brighten the day!'
Their yellow glow keeps the gray clouds at bay.

The tulips strike poses, red, pink, and gold,
Primping and preening, they're really quite bold.
With petals in action, they burst into song,
A cacophony of joy where all blossoms belong.

So gather around for this floral parade,
As the petals dance wildly in their grand charade.
In this garden of laughter, come join the delight,
For colors in bloom bring pure joy to the sight!

The Choir of Awakening Plants

In the heart of the garden, a choir takes flight,
Singing sweet songs in the morning light.
The blossoms all gather, a whimsical bunch,
To serenade sunbeams, and laugh over lunch.

The ivy chimes in with a leafy refrain,
While ferns sway their arms, feeling no pain.
'We're awakening now, what a joyous start!'
As each little sprout shows off its art.

The radishes roll, saying, 'Let's have some fun!'
While peas in their pods make sure they've won.
With roots all a-tumble and stems in a waltz,
The plants throw a party for all of their pals.

With laughter and voices that tickle the air,
This choir of greens brings a jubilant flair.
So dance with the plants, let your worries take flight,
For in this grand garden, everything's bright!

The Composition of Life Beneath

In the soil, the bass lines grow,
Worms wriggle, pulling to and fro.
Seeds giggle in their snug embrace,
Little sprouts make a funny face.

Raindrops tap like a crazy band,
Dancing plants in the warming sand.
With roots that twist, they all conspire,
Creating music that won't tire.

Fungi chiming in with a grin,
Breaking down the ick and sin.
Nature's pranksters, sprouting high,
Who knew dirt could sing and fly?

Listen close, the earth is sly,
With melodies that tickle the sky.
In every nook, the humor lurks,
Where life begins, and laughter works.

Foliage in Harmonious Motion

Leaves wiggle like they've lost their mind,
Swinging branches, one of a kind.
Even the weeds join in the dance,
Making gardeners take a chance.

A sunflower winks, a bit too bright,
While daisies joke through day and night.
The wind plays tricks, a cheeky tune,
Making plants sway like a loony balloon.

Butterflies wear polka dots with style,
They flap and flap, but just for a while.
Petals whisper secrets to the breeze,
Bumbling bees join in with ease.

Every inch, a giggle here,
Nature's laughter, loud and clear.
In this green world, oh what fun,
A jaunty tune for everyone!

Garden Medley of the Awakening

Sprouts peek out, all wide-eyed,
Every leaf like a youthful bride.
Petty arguments in the patch,
Who gets sunlight? Oh, what a catch!

Onions cry, they can't stand the heat,
While radishes cheer with a rooty beat.
Gardeners chuckle, tools in hand,
As veggies unite to make a stand.

Spinach dons a cape and flies,
Racing through the morning skies.
The carrots hide, they fear the stew,
This garden life is funny too!

Every bulb and stem takes part,
In nature's play, a quirky art.
With laughter bursting from the ground,
In the greenhouse, joy is found.

The Unraveling Notes of Time

Through seasons' change, the greens appear,
Tickling the senses, bringing cheer.
As winter fades, a joyful sound,
Life spins in circles, up from the ground.

The broccolis wear crowns of frost,
While peas laugh, never feeling lost.
Each sunbeam shines, a playful spark,
Where roots and leaves leave their mark.

Beneath the chaos, life's a jig,
A polka dance, not too big.
Time unfurls with a wiggle and sway,
As weeds plan pranks on brighter days.

So raise a glass to the sprouting fool,
In this garden, let's all drool.
With laughter ringing, isn't it nice?
Nature's comedy, our strongest spice.

Flourishing Crescendo of Nature

In the garden where giggles bloom,
Carrots dance in a leafy room.
Radishes wear red, looking quite fine,
As peas jiggle, forming a line.

Frogs leap high, croaking in glee,
While worms slither, so wiggly free.
Bees buzz around, wearing a hat,
Tickling flowers, imagine that!

Cabbages sway, putting on a show,
With broccoli strutting all in a row.
The sun shines bright, casting a grin,
As nature's orchestra begins to spin.

All around, sprouts frolic and play,
In their quirky, funny ballet.
With every wiggle and every sway,
They bring joy to every day!

Vegetal Rhythms Underfoot

Roots tap dance in the cozy earth,
Celebrating life with vibrant mirth.
Leaves shake it off, catching a breeze,
Whispering secrets to the buzzing bees.

Underfoot, radishes plot and scheme,
In their underground world, it's a dream.
While tiny sprouts giggle in delight,
Playing hide-and-seek from dawn till night.

Turnips toss and tumble with glee,
Trying to outroll a bumblebee.
Lettuce is laughing, oh what a sight,
Joining the fun, just feeling right!

In the patch where laughter is sown,
Every chortle is highly grown.
Nature's rhythms, a jovial show,
In the garden, where joy will flow!

The Mosaic of Tender Transformations

Seeds crack open, a giggle begins,
As sprouts stretch out, shaking off sins.
Radical carrots peek out of the ground,
While sprouts sing, a silly sound.

A cabbage twirls, almost a whirl,
While beans climb high, giving a twirl.
Squash winks at corn, wearing a grin,
As the soil is tickled by jovial kin.

The landscape bursts with colors so bright,
As greens and yellows take off in flight.
Nature's palette, a funky mix,
Where every sprout has its own little tricks.

Little seedlings, humorous sprouts,
Celebrating life, laughing it out.
In this mosaic, joy leaps and sings,
As the garden thrives with funny things!

Gentle Harmonies of the Green Realm

In the green realm, sprouts giggle away,
Bouncing with joy, come what may.
Eggplants wear hats, looking quite dandy,
While lettuce does a dance that's quite handy.

Peas are all chatting, sharing their tales,
While strawberries blush as the sun prevails.
The beans twist and twirl in their tight little pods,
Making up stories that seem quite odd.

Every leaf rustles with laughter and cheer,
As nature sings melodies sweet to the ear.
Frolicsome roots are tapping their toes,
In the green realm where silly joy flows.

Here, every sprout is a quirky delight,
In their gentle harmonies, pure and light.
The vegetables join in, making a fuss,
As nature invites us to dance with them thus!

The Fertile Chant of the Earth

In a garden full of dreams,
The radishes have laughter,
They wiggle with glee and shout,
"We're ready for the rapture!"

The carrots wear a silly grin,
As they dance beneath the earth,
"We're the crunch in every bite,
Who knew we'd have such worth?"

The peas just love a gossip scene,
They whisper in the breeze,
"Did you hear the celery's joke?
It's ripe for a tease!"

The soil hums a goofy tune,
As worms do twisty spins,
In the dirt where joy abounds,
Oh, let the fun begin!

A Dance of the Seasonal Leaves

Autumn leaves in bright attire,
Twirl down to the ground,
They giggle as they drift along,
In a funny whirling sound.

Winter's flakes are sly and jest,
Tumbling through the air,
They tickle all the sleepy trees,
With a frosty little flare.

Spring blooms burst with chuckles sweet,
In colors all a-sway,
"We're fresh, we're fun, we're here to play,
Hooray for another day!"

Summer brings a sunshine laugh,
With daisies in a line,
They wink and nod, a cheerful sight,
"Let's bask, it's pool time!"

Petals Sing in Colorful Tune

In the meadow where colors burst,
Flowers jokingly collide,
"I'm the red, but what are you?
Oh dear, we're all bonafide!"

Butterflies join the flowery fun,
With wings that flutter and flap,
"You look pretty but I'm the best,
In this floral world map!"

The daisies crown the grassy queens,
With petals oh so bright,
"When we dance, the sun's our stage,
Isn't this just right?"

A bid to bees, come gather round,
With honeyed words, they tease,
"We'll make a buzz and sweeten this,
Nature's grand, hilarious fees!"

Unearthing the Melodies of Growth

Beneath the earth, the laughter brews,
As tiny seeds conspire,
"Let's sprout up and show our moves,
We'll twirl and never tire!"

The sunbeams glow with radiant chuckles,
Saying, "Hey there, leaves!"
"Don't block the light, let's have some fun,
Be silly, if you please!"

The roots do the cha-cha underground,
Grooving in their space,
"We support your leafy dreams,
We're the vital base!"

When the rains come pouring down,
They splash and make a scene,
"It's party time in every drop,
Oh, how we love the green!"

The Dance of Tender Shoots

Tiny leaves break through the ground,
Doing a jig, oh what a sound!
Roots are tap dancing, playful, spry,
Waving goodnight to clouds up high.

Worms are wiggling, keeping time,
Their moves are all so well-defined.
Butterflies join with flaps and flares,
As ladybugs get caught in snares.

Sunshine chuckles, casting rays,
While raindrops join in liquid praise.
Each green sprout spins and twirls around,
A stage where joy in soil is found.

Under the moon, the sprouts sway slow,
With whispers of wind, they steal the show.
It's a comedy of growth tonight,
Where every sprout brings pure delight!

Notes of Life in the Garden

Buds peek out with a silly grin,
Tickled by breezes, letting laughs in.
Chirping crickets provide the beat,
While ants march in with tiny feet.

Petunias prance, tulips are bright,
All participating in this light.
Daisies giggle, soft in the sun,
As beetles race, oh what fun!

Earthworms hum their earthy song,
Composing tales of things gone wrong.
In the dirt, laughter is found,
Where colorful blooms spin around.

Gathered dew drops glisten and play,
Singing together, come what may.
In this garden where quirks abound,
The funniest life can always be found!

Symphonic Awakening

Seeds are dreaming in a zany plot,
While donuts frolic in a hot pot.
Sprouting snickers as they unfurl,
Each tiny shoot gives life a twirl.

Frogs croak funny tunes, all around,
While the flowers spread joy profound.
Caterpillars munch in rhythmic spree,
As grasshoppers hop for comedic glee.

Sunflowers nod with wiggly heads,
Buds shake laughter instead of dreads.
Nature's humor blossoms, bright and bold,
In every petal, a joke is told.

So let's rejoice in the garden's throng,
Where veggies groove and critters belong.
Every sprout, a note in the air,
Creating a concert beyond compare!

Flourishing in Distant Harmony

Sprouts in rows with silly hats,
Chatting quietly with nearby cats.
Lettuce tickles the radish's ear,
In this garden, laughter is near.

The peas giggle, snapping away,
While beetroot jests at the end of the day.
Mice do the tango near the gate,
While the cosmos spins, isn't it great?

Every leaf tells a joke or two,
While roots beneath share secrets anew.
Squirrels are conducting sweet shenanigans,
Pushing sprigs into their funny plans.

So gather 'round, let's have a cheer,
For sprouts that sing, and jokes we hold dear.
In harmony, they romp and play,
Making gardens brighter every day!

Radiant Strings of Life

In gardens where the peas do dance,
They mingle with the beans, by chance.
With every twist and every turn,
They plot a path for sprouts to learn.

Tomatoes wear their playful hats,
While carrots engage in silly chats.
The cucumbers giggle with their friends,
As laughter in the soil extends.

Zucchinis play hide-and-seek in rows,
While radishes strike funny poses,
This merry band of veggies sings,
With sprouting joy, plankton springs.

So join the fun, don't be shy,
As leafy laughter fills the sky.
With the sun as our shining mime,
We grow in rhythm, one sprout at a time.

Prelude to Verdant Dreams

A dance begins on sunny leaves,
The broccoli twirls and gently weaves.
Spinach hums a tune so light,
While beets declare it's veggie night.

Peppers strut with colors bright,
Dressed up for spring's fanciful flight.
Onions giggle, shedding tears,
For roots of joy outshine their fears.

Lettuce rolls in leafy spirals,
While radish pranks make lively trials.
The garden band plays without rest,
In this rooty realm, all feel blessed.

So join the revelry, laugh along,
In green attire, we all belong.
The soil's chuckle, the sun's warm beam,
Unfolds a bright and verdant dream.

The Soundtrack of Earth's Renewal

In the earth, a hidden groove,
As sprouts emerge, they start to move.
A symphony of greens unfold,
With every story waiting to be told.

Seeds in rows, they tap and spin,
The carrots hope for gold to win.
While radish roots sing 'Follow me!',
Beneath the soil, a jubilee.

Cabbages nod to the rhythm's cheer,
With every sprout, the spring draws near.
As nature plays its quirky tune,
We dance like leaves beneath the moon.

So grab your spoons and pots with glee,
Join in the playful harmony!
For in the earth, we find our song,
A joyful tune where we belong.

Soundscapes of Springtime Growth

The daisies chatter, quite a scene,
While violets strut, all dressed in green.
A trumpet sound from ladybugs,
As insects dance in tiny hugs.

Sprouts emerge to play their part,
With sunlit smiles that steal the heart.
The whispers of the breeze, so fun,
Guide each leafy laugh under the sun.

In the depths, where roots entwine,
A banter forms from every vine.
As nature's orchestra takes its cue,
The audience, a rabbit or two.

So let's enjoy this lively scene,
Where greenery and giggles glean.
In this patch of life, bright and spry,
We're one big family, watch us fly!

Harmonies in the Soil

In the garden where greens frolic,
Tiny radishes dance in a row.
Carrots hum a tune that's nostalgic,
While peas in a pod steal the show.

Worms wiggle in their own little beat,
Giving every seed a good shimmy.
Sunflowers laugh at their funky feet,
As chalky dreams become quite filmy.

Broccoli joins with a headstrong twist,
Zucchini struts, oh what a sight!
With tiny sprouts that can't resist,
And kale in shades of green delight.

Together they grow, with gusto and cheer,
A leafy orchestra, wet with dew.
Nature's oddballs, we hold them dear,
As plants conduct a wacky revue.

Buds and Beats

Buds of lettuce, dressed to impress,
They shimmy and shake in their beds of dirt.
Radish circles, garnished with finesse,
Movin' and groovin', never to hurt.

Tomatoes roll in a salsa spree,
While peppers pop like a bubbly tune.
Cucumbers bending, carefree as can be,
Under the bright, mischievous moon.

Chard in the corner throws a dance fit,
With leafy arms reaching high in the air.
Every sprout gets its chance to commit,
To a jolly, green, rooty affair.

So grab your trowel, let's have some fun,
In this quirky garden of jabber and jest.
Plant a giggle, watch laughter run,
With beats from the earth, we're truly blessed!

The Conductor of Budding Life

In the garden's stage, the maestro grins,
A carrot baton in hand, so spry.
With radishes wiggling, he begins,
To lead the concert of seedlings nigh.

The beans in the back are just a bit shy,
But join in the chorus, waving their leaves,
While tulips follow, reaching for the sky,
In a whimsical dance, the soil believes.

As onions peek out in a bulbous cheer,
Lettuce twirls in a light summer breeze.
Every sprout plays their part loud and clear,
Creating a melody that's meant to please.

As evening falls, the cheers start to swell,
With roots intertwining, a bustling crowd.
In this garden circus, all is well,
Echoing laughter, exuberant and loud.

Crescendos from the Earth

A serenade rises from the ground,
As peas and beans harmonize in delight.
With prancing radish, the laughter's profound,
They twirl and they spin, oh what a sight!

Cauliflower nods, all dressed in white,
While carrots strut in their orange best.
The choir of sprouts brings pure delight,
Each plant plays its role; they're truly blessed.

Broccoli breathes deep, takes a big bow,
As tiny sprouts cheer, rallying around.
They laugh in unison, "Look at us now!"
With chuckles that echo into the ground.

The moon rises high, joining the fun,
Casting its glow on this green jubilee.
As sprouts take a bow, the concert's not done,
For the earth holds a rhythm for all to see!

Rhythms in the Rain

Raindrops tap dance on the ground,
Little sprouts bounce all around.
A giggle from a blade so green,
Wiggling like a silly queen.

Puddles form a splashy stage,
Sprouts perform, as if engaged.
With every drip, a laugh is made,
In this wet and wild parade.

Soil squishes like a soft pie,
While worms wiggle and pass by.
Bouncing beans do twist and shout,
In their cozy, muddy bout.

After rain, the sun comes out,
Sprouts prance high without a doubt.
Nature's band now takes the lead,
In a funny, leafy creed.

Rooted Resilience

Down below, where roots entwine,
Plant pals share some punch lines.
Feeling brave, they wiggle tight,
Telling tales of shroomy fright.

A radish thinks it's quite the star,
But carrots know just who they are.
With leafy hats and roots of gold,
They trade wisecracks, brave and bold.

Through storms and winds, they hold their place,
Laughing hard, they join the race.
"Grow up!" says one to a nearby bean,
"Don't you know what I mean?"

With every stretch and upward shot,
They keep their humor, never rot.
Life's a giggle in the dirt,
With even thorns dressed in a skirt.

Vibrations of Verdant Life

In the garden, grasshoppers sing,
While daisies dance and bumblebees cling.
A worm throws a party deep down low,
"Come one, come all! Let's put on a show!"

The daisies sway with laughter bright,
Claiming they're taller, full of delight.
"Your stems are short, but bless your heart,
At least you know how to do your part!"

With a chuckle, cabbage rolls by,
Sporting a hat—oh my, oh my!
Radical radishes join in the spree,
Rooting for each other, wild and free.

Life's a concert of greens and glee,
In this funny world, just let it be.
Every sprout has a note to play,
In nature's orchestra, come what may.

Sowing the Soundtrack

With every seed that hits the earth,
A tune begins, oh what a birth!
Compost choir sings a funny song,
While daisies dance and roots grow long.

Funny fungi join the mix,
Mushroom jokes are a real fix.
They tell a tale of underground,
Of friends above who bounce around.

Plant pals throw a shindig bright,
Sowing seeds into the night.
"Let's grow big!" squeaks tiny corn,
"I'll be a stalk until the morn!"

As the harvest moon shines high,
Sprouts giggle, reaching for the sky.
In this garden, joy's the track,
With roots that wiggle and never lack.

Nature's Crescendo

In a patch of dirt, a tiny seed,
Danced with joy, oh what a deed!
Wiggling roots and leaves so spry,
Chasing butterflies that flutter by.

The sun burst in with a cheeky grin,
Tickling sprouts beneath their skin.
They giggled at the rain's soft splat,
As worms joined in to share the chat.

The daisies donned their finest hats,
While snails played tune on swinging mats.
Bees buzzed tunes quite out of key,
But oh, how lovely was their spree!

And as the moon cast a glance so sly,
The garden held a midnight spy.
With crickets chirping a jazzy throw,
Even the blushing tomato seeds danced low.

The Awakening Garden

In a sleepy patch, the sprouts did yawn,
Stretching their leaves, the day was born.
A worm wiggled past with a big ol' grin,
As clovers giggled, "Oh, let's begin!"

The radishes rolled in a game of tag,
While the sunflowers swayed in a jaunty rag.
With roots in the air like they just don't care,
Their leafy shenanigans caused quite a scare!

Behold the peas with their witty jokes,
Telling tales of sprouted folks.
With laughter echoing through the plot,
Even the weeds joined, giving all they've got!

As dusk arrived with a sleepy sigh,
The garden whispered its lullaby.
In nature's mad parade, they took their bows,
Stars twinkled down, demanding applause.

Melodies of Green Growth

In the morning light, seeds danced awake,
With laughter rising like a loopy quake.
Carrots juggled while peas did sway,
Who knew plants could have such a play?

Basil and thyme held a cooking show,
While potatoes amazed with their funky flow.
Tomatoes rolled in like a bunch of clowns,
Spreading giggles through the leafy towns.

Butterflies twirled in soft ballet,
In a garden where whimsy came out to play.
With bees on drums, they formed a band,
Nature's ruckus, perfectly unplanned!

As the sun took a bow behind the trees,
The garden cozied up in a gentle breeze.
With dreams of rainbows and starlit cheer,
They settled in for a night of cheer.

Whispers of the Seedlings

Tiny whispers in the soil below,
"Who's got the scoop?" "I don't know!"
A sprout peeked up, feeling quite bold,
"Let's swap our tales, they never get old!"

The radishes giggled with stories of roots,
While celery shared tales of life in suits.
Peas made puns that rolled with ease,
While carrots joked, "I'm the best of these!"

A sunflower waved with a bright sunny face,
Claiming it held the perfect grace.
They all agreed in a happy roar,
"Let's grow together, who could ask for more?"

As twilight arrived, they shared a joke,
Until a fox sneezed and sent them up the yoke.
Laughter echoed as they tucked in tight,
Dreaming of fun till morning light.

The Dreamscape of Budding Life

In the garden, life takes flight,
Tiny sprouts in morning light.
With giggles from the soil below,
They sprout up high, putting on a show.

Chasing worms in leafy streams,
Hopping high on leafy dreams.
A parade of green, they prance about,
Making sure no doubt's about.

Sunshine giggles, rain clouds cheer,
As seedlings toast with roots in beer.
A sprout with shades, oh isn't he grand?
As dandelions dance to the band!

In the breeze, they sway and bow,
Creating magic, here and now.
With a wink and playful jig,
These cheeky greens are oh-so-big!

Flourishing with the Wind's Whispers

Beneath the whispering willow tree,
Sprouts giggle in harmony.
They trade their secrets with the breeze,
While teasing ladybugs with ease.

Each tiny leaf a witty jest,
In a leaf-off, they sure are blessed.
A radish giggles, 'Can you beat me?'
While carrots dream of being free!

With every rustle of the green,
A tale of laughter goes unseen.
The wind sings them a playful tune,
As daisies dance beneath the moon.

Old gnomes watch with a knowing grin,
At mischief sprouting from within.
In this tiller's merry abode,
Life's punchlines sprout and explode!

New Beginnings in Rooted Harmony

Sprouts awaken from their sleep,
In a tangled dance, they leap.
With roots entwined, they share a laugh,
As earthworms join their leafy staff.

"What's that noise? A beetle race!"
"Not bad for a small green place!"
Giggles echo through the soil,
In this realm of leafy toil.

The beets wear hats, the peas wear shoes,
Each sprout has its own funny muse.
With beaming smiles, they march in line,
Like veggies caught on a punchy vine!

Slipping 'round in muddy glee,
Building castles, one, two, three.
In this vibrant, silly scene,
What a sight to grow so green!

Orchestrating Nature's Palette

A sunflower conductor takes the stage,
With a baton made of a twig and sage.
The sprouts sway like a quirky choir,
Each note sung higher, never to tire.

Carrots tap dance, beets do the twist,
While radishes make a funky list.
In leafy outfits, they strut with flair,
Giggling sprouts beyond compare!

Oh, what a ruckus, the garden sings,
As butterflies flaunt their vibrant wings.
While bumblebees buzz and play the tune,
The orchestra blooms beneath the moon.

And when the sun comes back around,
The sprouts take a bow, oh how profound!
In the garden's show, no doubts arise,
For laughter sprouts and never dies!

Arpeggios of the Undergrowth

In the soil, a dance begins,
Tiny roots play hide and seek,
Carrot tops wear leafy grins,
And broccoli starts to squeak.

With a wiggle and a shake,
Mushrooms burst with bubbly glee,
Radishes play a silly prank,
Chasing ladybugs with glee.

Beans are climbing up the trellis,
Chorus lines of green and tall,
Peas are singing like a fellas,
Messy laughter fills the hall.

In the patch, the veggies boast,
Onions put on their best smirk,
Cucumbers throw a tiny toast,
As carrots sway, they go berserk!

The Garden's Secret Symphony

Underneath a leafy cloak,
A melody of sprigs unfolds,
Beets hum softly, while they choke,
As cabbage starts its tale so bold.

Tomatoes twirl in shiny red,
Their juicy notes a burst of flair,
Zucchini does a flipping spread,
While peppers dance without a care.

Radish roots tap out a beat,
As peas pirouette on high,
Quirky rhythms, quite the treat,
In a jolly garden sigh.

With worms that wiggle in the dirt,
The flowers sway to the fun tune,
In this patch where mischief's flirt,
Every sprout hums under the moon!

Flourish and Flourish

Sprouts are plotting something grand,
They whisper secrets with a grin,
Carrots cheering, "Take a stand!"
As broccoli declares a spin.

Lettuce leads the leafy crew,
Dancing wildly in the breeze,
Cabbage spins, "We'll dance for you!"
And radishes aim to tease.

Dandelions, bold and bright,
Challenge flowers to a duel,
With petals floating like a kite,
It's hard to tell who's the fool.

Seeds are sneaking from their beds,
With tiny feet and giggle fits,
In this garden known for threads,
They plot to pull off silly skits!

From Seedling to Serenade

In a tiny pot, a seed did dream,
To sprout and sing a happy song,
Watered by a sunbeam's beam,
It chuckled, "I can't be wrong!"

Through the dirt, it pushed with zest,
With each wiggle, it took its shot,
Worms cheered loudly, "You're the best!"
As lettuce joined, "We'll have a lot!"

Daisies laughed, "What's that you grew?"
"Just a little leafy charm,"
While carrots quipped, "We're proud of you!"
In this garden full of warm.

As sprouts began their lively spree,
Butterflies joined in the fun,
Nature's band, so wild and free,
Singing songs until they're done!

The Ballet of Sprouting Tenderness

In a garden where greens come awake,
Tiny dancers perform, make no mistake.
With twirls and hops, they spring from the earth,
Each little sprout claims its quirky worth.

The cabbage leads with a pirouette,
While radishes giggle; they're not done yet.
An audience of weeds taps its feet,
As sunbeams bounce to the rhythm, so sweet.

With every move, the peas swing in cheer,
A ballet of laughter for everyone near.
Broccoli bows, with a tip of its crown,
The garden's stage calls for joy, not a frown!

So twirl and sway with the green troupe around,
In this leafy ballet, pure fun will abound.
Nature's jesters leap with zest so grand,
In the freshest of shows, they're in high demand!

Rhythms of Roots and Dreams

Beneath the soil, the roots play a tune,
Strumming the secrets of morning's bright moon.
They wiggle and giggle, a rooty ballet,
Composing a melody, hip-hip-hooray!

Zucchini and onions join in the fray,
While mushrooms beat drums in a funky display.
A rhythm of growth where the laughter is thick,
These underground parties know all the right tricks.

Beets start a conga, carrots join in,
With every groove, they embrace the spin.
Rhythms of life, both silly and grand,
In this earthen club, they take a bold stand.

The sprightly potatoes start tap-dancing too,
To the roots' rhythm, they know just what to do.
With dreams being planted deep down in the muck,
This raucous root jam just has all the luck!

The Song of Sunlit Sprouts

From the earth, they pop with a giggly grin,
Swaying to the sunshine, let the fun begin.
Each little sprout sings its own merry tune,
Beneath the bright sky, afternoon in June.

Tomatoes belt out a high-pitched refrain,
While beans do the boogie, feeling no pain.
Peas blow raspberries; their jokes make us chuckle,
In this vibrant garden, every heart's a buckle!

The sunflowers sway, conducting the show,
With petals like fans, they put on a glow.
Spinach chimes in with a leafy little back,
And soon all the sprouts form a merry pack.

As laughter unfurls in the warm balmy air,
The song of the sprouts fills the garden with flair.
So let's dance along and join in the fun,
Singing with sprouts till the day's finally done!

Festivities of the Blooming World

In the blooming world, it's a party today,
Where flowers don hats, and the sun leads the way.
A riot of colors spreads laughter and cheer,
As petals in bright shades bring all of us near.

Tulips break dance with a flair and a twirl,
Pansies and daisies give each other a whirl.
The lilacs are gossiping, fond of their style,
As fragrant confetti floats down for a while.

The garden's abuzz with a buzzing delight,
While bumblebees toast to a sweet nectar night.
Every blossom bursts with a quirky say-so,
In costumes of pollen, they steal every show!

With wind as the DJ, the blooms prance around,
Each stem getting groovy to that buzzing sound.
In this jovial fiesta, we're all in the mix,
Floating on laughter, no reason for tricks!

www.ingramcontent.com/pod-product-compliance
Lightning Source LLC
Chambersburg PA
CBHW070311120526
44590CB00017B/2628